AF413508

10

PATHS TO UNCOVER WELLNESS

JS KUMAR

INDIA • SINGAPORE • MALAYSIA

ISBN 979-8-89632-445-4

Index

Dedication

To my Mom & Dad,

To my wife, Mausmi,

To my son Bhargv,

To my family and friends, for your unwavering support and encouragement,

To my coach and mentors, for your wisdom and guidance,

and

To the readers, for your curiosity and imagination,

I'm immensely grateful that this book is in your hands.

Acknowledgment

This book is drawn from my health journal, reflecting what I've learned, practiced, and consistently followed in my daily routine. It would not have come to life without the support of incredible individuals. I owe heartfelt thanks to many generous people who made its completion possible with their contributions.

I sincerely thank my family for their invaluable assistance as team members. I want to extend my sincere appreciation to my family. In addition to supporting me, they have also been exceptional teammates. Their unwavering assistance has functioned as a stabilizing force, bolstering my determination and shifting my focus toward the primary goal: fulfilling my life's mission.

Furthermore, I feel deeply grateful to my furry friend, Happy. His constant companionship has been a boundless source of encouragement and joy throughout the research and writing process. His presence ensured I went to bed on time and woke up naturally, without needing an alarm.

Preface

Until the first quarter of 2023, my weight in my early forties fluctuated at approximately 225 pounds, which categorized me as obese. As a result, I experienced acute knee pain, an obese liver, and elevated cholesterol levels, with my blood sugar levels precariously close to the threshold. The unpredictable work hours, higher expectations, and deadlines to meet the targets significantly impacted my personal and professional lives.

During an executive program at Harvard Medical School, I learned the 6 basic pillars of lifestyle medicine. It's a holistic approach to enhancing overall health and well-being.

I realized the importance of mental peace for the success of these foundations and aimed for a balanced work-life. Weight loss emerged as the primary solution to my health issues, which, in turn, led me to embrace the entirety of the 6 pillars of lifestyle medicine.

The 6 pillars of lifestyle medicine—a whole-food and plant-predominant dietary pattern, physical activity, restorative sleep, stress management, avoidance of risky substances, and positive social connections—are implemented.

By thoroughly examining hydration-rich foods, antioxidants, micronutrients, and macronutrients, I developed a systematic approach to dietary selection. I adopted a vegetarian diet and incorporated plant-based proteins to promote muscle growth and recovery. I also established a consistent fitness regimen consisting of cardiovascular exercises, strength training, and high-intensity interval training for more than 180 minutes per week. Through this nutritious regimen, which excludes intermittent fasting, I have achieved a body weight of around 180 pounds, but intermittent fasting is good for your body's metabolic rate.

However, the COVID-19 pandemic increased awareness of the significance of good health and robust immune systems. Furthermore, it emphasized the importance of familial and relational bonds, which influenced a transformation in my career opportunities in the final phase. This modification increased happiness when spending time with family and friends, and a more harmonious work-life balance, ultimately contributing to a life devoid of tension.

Acknowledging my significant role in my family, workplace, and professional spheres, I resolved to exercise deliberate self-control over my behavior. Having achieved a harmonious equilibrium between professional and personal life, my attention is now directed toward the fundamental principles of lifestyle medicine. Having achieved positive health outcomes through years of diligent effort, I am now resolved to combat obesity and reverse the aging process by adhering to these guiding principles.

During Phase 1, I cultivated a preference for nutrient-dense foods, improved my knowledge of micronutrients and macronutrients, and prioritized cooking with health in mind over personal preference. In addition, to individual training and maintaining gym memberships, I implemented physical activities such as walking with my dog and relocating my parking distance from the workplace.

Transitioning to Phase 2, I prioritized maintaining positive social connections by attending frequent home visits and regular meetings with friends, family, and colleagues. The central theme of stress resilience was resolving workplace and relationship tensions. Developing a practice of practical meditation and decreasing caffeine consumption emerged as strategic approaches to enhance stress management.

Hazardous substances such as alcohol, cigarettes, and shisha were deliberately avoided. Alcohol consumption was limited to occasional, event-based instances. These adjustments signify a fresh start, substantially enhancing physical well-being, and dramatically improving health.

I've strictly adhered to my well-balanced diet plan for the past few months/years, losing approximately 50 lbs of body fat. I incorporate all 6 pillars of lifestyle and wellness into my daily routine. Typically, I start my day with hydration, rising at 5 a.m. for a vigorous 45-minute walk with my dog, "Happy." My breakfast consists of nutritious grains such as oats, millets, or granules combined with citrus fruits or berries.

Around 10:30 a.m., I have a bowl of seasonal fruits like papaya, mango, apple, banana, kiwi, or watermelon, depending on what is available in the market. I eat a salad bowl with homemade dressings 30 minutes before lunch to complete it by 2:00 p.m. In the late afternoon, usually between 4:00 and 4:30 p.m., I eat a handful of almonds or walnuts. I prefer a soup made with green-boiled vegetables in the evening or a green salad dressed in lemon and black pepper. I have maintained my hydration level between 2.5 and 3.0L of water; however, this decreases when traveling.

This food pattern is steady throughout the week, with just minor deviations on weekends. Despite the little changes, fruits and salads are always a part of my meals, although in smaller quantities.

The basic formula for weight loss is a calorie deficit, which means that your calorie intake must be less than the number of calories you burn. Losing around 50 lbs inspired me to write a book and share with our readers the knowledge on how to lose weight without a strict diet or intermittent fasting. Weight loss is certainly feasible, but you must be consistent and work on your lifestyle and the other 6 foundations listed above. So, if you want to succeed as a self-coach, follow these 10 paths to uncover wellness, and one thing, your health is a top priority, and you are solely responsible for it.

Chapter 1

Discovering Your Purpose: The Anchor for a Meaningful Life

Living a happy and satisfied life is a prerequisite for overall well-being, and it is made possible by being in excellent health. It encourages mental clarity, emotional stability, and physical exercise. In addition, good health reduces the likelihood of illness, boosts productivity, and enhances quality of life.

But, what is good health?

Good health is a state of complete physical, mental, and social well-being, not merely the absence of disease or disability. The World Health Organization (WHO) defines health holistically.

- Physical well-being is the state in which the body and its organs usually function. It addresses nutrition, exercise, rest, and avoiding harmful substances.

- Mental Well-being: Emotional stability, cognitive function, and managing stress and challenges are all signs of healthy mental health. It involves being mentally strong, maintaining healthy relationships, and maintaining an optimistic view.

- Social Well-being: This aspect emphasizes the importance of a supportive social network, relationships, and a loving neighborhood. A person who is in good health not only has a happy social life, but also excellent physical and mental well-being.

A combination of preventive measures, healthcare access, and lifestyle choices is often required to achieve and sustain optimal health. Developing and maintaining healthful routines, including consistent physical activity, a well-balanced diet, stress management, and medical checkups, is imperative. In addition, factors including environment, genetics, and socioeconomic status can impact an individual's overall health.

It's important to remember that exceptional health is not a set situation that changes from person to person, but a dynamic, continual process. A positive outlook, regular self-care, and healthy habits contribute to overall well-being.

It's essential to maintain excellent health for several reasons:

- Health determines a person's total level of physical well-being. It ensures that every organ and system functions correctly and allows the body to function at its peak.

- Good health significantly enhances one's quality of life. It enables people to engage in various activities and hobbies, and enjoy life without being limited by health issues.

- A healthy lifestyle has been linked to higher productivity. Individuals in good physical condition are more likely to be productive at work or when performing daily tasks.

- Staying healthy can prevent many illnesses. Regular exercise, a balanced diet, and enough sleep can help prevent numerous medical conditions.

- The state of one's mind and body is closely related. Regular exercise and a well-balanced diet can lift one's spirits and reduce the likelihood of mental health issues, like depression and anxiety.

- Good health is often associated with a longer lifespan. Proper self-care can lead to a longer, healthier life.

- Being in good health makes it easier to make new friends, engage in social interactions, build relationships, and participate in community events.

- Being sick can lead to higher medical expenses and lower productivity. However, individual and community health can impact economic well-being.

In conclusion, as health impacts all aspects of well-being, including mental, social, and physical fitness, it is crucial for living a happy and productive life.

The following are some health-related extended excuses for working professionals or students between the ages of 20 and 46, and we don't mind resolving it. Consider this as part of our lifestyle:

1. Sitting for extended amounts of time at your desk.

2. Unable to work out or practice yoga or any other activities.

3. Eating practices and irregular digestion.

4. Daily intake of excessive amounts of tea or coffee.

5. Overindulging in alcohol.

6. Effects of continuing to host parties and festivities late into the night.

7. Not drinking enough water to stay healthy overall.

8. Uncontrol excessive screen time to enhance psychological well-being.

9. Conflicts in relationships, particularly those involving a spouse, siblings, etc.

10. Smoking as a coping mechanism or a status symbol.

11. Excessive driving.

12. Low Focus and demotivation for personal growth.

13. Stress to lose weight.

14. Being overweight or fat all of one's life.

15. Experiencing frequent fever or the typical flu attacks.

16. Poor immune system and more.

17. Individuals who are conscious of their careers are eager to demonstrate their full potential.

The list is extensive, but these are the predominant ones that are widespread among most of us. Now, the big question is:

Q1. What would you like to change in your life?

Q2. What motivates you to make this change?

Q3. What is your plan of action for making the change?

Chapter 2

The Power of Connection: Building and Nurturing Social Relationships

Social interaction is as essential to human survival as food, water and shelter. Without social connections, an individual's health and lifespan are drastically reduced.

- An increased risk of heart disease, stroke, hypertension, diabetes, anxiety, depression, and dementia is linked to poor or inadequate social connections.

- Increased vulnerability to respiratory infections and viruses,

- Reduced academic success and lower job performance.

Developing stronger social ties can be a proactive strategy for leading a happy and satisfied life. It can improve job performance, personal satisfaction and educational success. Additionally, it can help create more robust, safer and wealthier communities that are more closely knit.

Human Beings are sociable animals; socializing cannot begin until there is a shared goal. You can achieve a shared goal by drawing them in with a specific interest. "Food" is where this particular interest begins. Discussing food without mentioning friends, family, and culture is impossible. The social-ecological model of transformation is helpful to know. As much as it is about the food, sharing meals with family is about building social bonds. Food serves as a bridge. There are numerous occasions during the day when we get together with family, friends, coworkers, and others. These occasions include having coffee or tea in the morning, lunch meetings, dinner with family, holiday suppers, celebrating, and cooking together. Such occasions bring the chances for interaction.

Cooking has a higher tendency to follow a healthy diet. The important people are family and friends. Studies have indicated that individuals who prepare dinner at home daily eat a better diet. Individuals take their time selecting oils, spices, herbs, and other ingredients. These dinners are the result of careful planning and work. It can be enjoyable, and there is ownership. Small gestures like this foster close bonds and relationships, enabling them to support one another emotionally and socially. Undoubtedly, the individuals in our social circles impact the foods we eat. Our goal is to blend in.

Nicholas Christakis and James Fowler's book, *Connected*, delves thoroughly into social networks. Additionally, their research was published in The New England Journal of Medicine, one of the top medical journals. They stated, "A person's chances of becoming obese increase if he or she had a friend who became obese in a given interval." This demonstrates how our friends can inexplicably impact us, even if we don't socialize or dine with them regularly.

In a Ted Talk, James Fowler states that he shed five pounds after realizing that his weight could affect the weight of his son, his son's friend, and the mother of his son's friend. You may acquire weight if a buddy of yours gains weight. James Fowler advises that if you want to change for the better, involve your friends and family.

In conclusion, surround yourself with loved ones who encourage you to follow a healthy diet and may even be traveling this path with you. Recognize that many people can look up to you as a leader and role model. Never forget that what we do affects those around us.

Examine this instance now: Restaurant patrons' food choices may be influenced by peer pressure.

Studies recommend that you surround yourself with companions who make good food choices if you wish to eat healthier when dining out. According to a survey conducted by the University of Illinois, individuals who dine in groups and are required to declare their meal decisions out loud typically choose from the same menu categories. According to Ellison, the study's main finding is that people were happy when they made decisions comparable to those seated nearby. "I am happier, or at least less dissatisfied, if I eat higher-calorie foods and spend more money if my peers are ordering higher-calorie foods or spending more money." The first person to place an order at a restaurant where we eat out typically sets the tone. According to research, when restaurant individuals place comparable orders as their friends, they feel good about themselves. Have you noticed that if the first person at the table orders a salad, then it's quite likely that other people will order salads as well? Someone else may get dessert if someone concludes the meal with it. Others are unlikely to order dessert if nobody raises the subject or if someone says, "No, no, thank you, I won't have any," right away.

In my understanding, around 75% of the people in our immediate social circle impact our physical and mental health. If those around you do not support you in your weight reduction and maintenance, then either you gain their support or your motivation is destroyed.

In these situations, you must be resolute in your choice and allow yourself to mirror your changes to help them overcome their mental obstacles. The saying "nothing is impossible, as long as you start with I".

This serves as a reminder that humans are social beings and that we need to consider the social-ecological model of change when considering ourselves or our clients. In this model, we are in the center, with our immediate family, coworkers, and neighborhood surrounding and impacting us. Beyond that, our state's policies and laws, as well as those of our city, continue to have an impact on us. Of course, there is also the nation. The family we grew up in, our immediate area, our place of employment, the social norms, and the regulations and laws of our city, state, and nation all influence our eating habits.

Choosing healthy foods is crucial to building and maintaining relationships with parents, siblings, and other family members. Mealtimes are a customary and essential time for family members to connect, talk, and support one another. A few examples of how eating behaviors foster the growth of relationships between parents and siblings are as follows:

- Spending time together over meals is an excellent way to create memories with your family. It makes a dedicated space for family members to bond and catch up on each other's lives.

- Cooking or choosing meals according to family members' tastes is one way to demonstrate love and care for them. It also shows consideration for their nutritional needs and preferences.

- Family meals contribute to the development of traditions. These shared meals—holiday feasts, monthly dinners, or special occasions—become cherished traditions that strengthen the bonds within the family over time.

- Meals provide a relaxed setting for conversation and friendship. Whether for breakfast, lunch, or dinner, sharing meals with family members fosters communication and allows them to share thoughts, emotions, and experiences.

- Encouraging and modeling a nutritious diet within the family aids in forming healthy eating habits in children and younger siblings. It promotes a shared commitment to health and well-being.

- Food is usually associated with celebrations. Having a special supper to celebrate accomplishments, anniversaries, and birthdays fosters enjoyment and community.

- Sharing a meal together helps promote a calm environment for settling conflicts. Families that eat meals together can better overcome issues and talk honestly because they get closer.

- Taking turns in the kitchen or participating in meal planning can promote a sense of reciprocity, fostering shared responsibility for the happiness and well-being of each family member.

- Many priceless memories are associated with having meals together as a family. These meals create a collective memory within the family, whether it's a treasured recipe passed down through the years or an extraordinary holiday feast.

To sum up, a family's dietary decisions can be a powerful tool for building and strengthening connections. They create a foundation for communication, exhibit love and care, and create enduring family traditions and memories. Family members who share meals grow to feel very connected to one another.

The family serves as a crucial foundation for your transformation; if they resist or do not support it, the transformation becomes challenging, and you will face a repelling effect from various directions. For example, when I started my journey, it was difficult for my family to cope with the requirements. My wife needed to prepare 3 meals: one for my son, one for herself, and one for me. Later, we standardized the process and timings.

Now, let's explore another aspect: how your weight loss journey will generate value or impact the environment of your friends.

Eating habits can significantly influence the development and maintenance of friendships. Sharing meals is a social and cultural custom that promotes intimacy and togetherness. Discover how your eating habits affect the growth of relationships and how friendly you are in maintaining your friendship. Are you making all 10 points clear, or deviating from them? Check it now.

Sr. No	Created Value	Impact Yes/No
1	By trying new meals and dining at different restaurants, friends might discover more about one another's origins. It provides an opportunity to learn about each other's preferences, histories and cultures.	
2	Happy memories are frequently associated with mealtime gatherings. Creating enduring memories through routine meals or big occasion festivities strengthens bonds.	
3	Food can break boundaries and create a warm environment. During dinner, people can open up and feel more comfortable with one another, resulting in deeper, and more meaningful conversations.	

Sr. No	Created Value	Impact Yes/No
4	Selecting and enjoying meals together results in shared experiences. Engaging in such activities as cooking, dining at new restaurants, or exchanging favored dishes fosters the development of stronger friendships.	
5	Making a meal that satisfies a friend's dietary requirements or preferences is an effort to demonstrate thought and care. It shows how much you value and care about their well-being.	
6	Talking over meals with friends can help build trust. Eating together is often seen as a symbol of friendship and trust, fostering peace and understanding.	
7	Food is usually associated with celebrations. Whether it's a birthday, a career advancement, or any other achievement, celebrating these moments over dinner helps to strengthen connections.	
8	Dinners provide a cozy setting for friendly conversation. Whether at a lunch meeting, dinner party, or just over coffee, sharing food is a terrific way to promote genuine and meaningful communication.	
9	Meal sharing that is reciprocated creates a give-and-take dynamic that benefits relationships. Friends who alternate hosting or treating each other to dinners, develop a harmonious and encouraging relationship.	
10	Creating a schedule for meals together facilitates regular interaction, giving people a reason to get together. Friendships become habitual, allowing them to stay in touch and be involved in each other's lives.	
Total Score (out of 10)		

What we eat says a lot about our personalities and capacity to establish and preserve friendships. Sharing meals deepens and strengthens connections for special occasions, culinary adventures, or regular meals.

Several additional factors relate to social influence. Let's delve into another significant one: the workplace, office, school, university, etc.

Eating habits can impact establishing and maintaining relationships with coworkers, particularly in work environments that encourage social interaction. Sharing meals or snacks might lead to opportunities for teamwork and bonding. Some ways that eating habits can help to establish relationships with coworkers are as follows, but embracing a healthy diet within a group may pose challenges as you move forward.

Sr. No	Created Value	Impact Yes/No
1	Having dinner or a coffee break together might be an informal way for colleagues to network. It enables people to meet one another outside of formal professional contexts, have casual conversations and strengthen their sense of community.	
2	Organizing meals or snacks for the group fosters solidarity and collaboration. It allows colleagues to relax, socialize and create healthy relationships that enhance cooperation and teamwork.	
3	Food is usually associated with celebrations. Sharing meals or bringing in treats to celebrate birthdays, anniversaries, and successes fosters a supportive and upbeat work environment.	

Sr. No	Created Value	Impact Yes/No
4	Having lunch together can be a terrific opportunity to start a conversation, especially with new coworkers or during team-building exercises. It encourages candid dialogue and a more relaxed atmosphere.	
5	Eating choices can help celebrate diversity in the workplace. Coordinating multi-cuisine potluck meals, or other gatherings, allows colleagues to discuss their cultural preferences and histories.	
6	Expressing gratitude to coworkers can be as easy as bringing lunch, snacks, or candies. Letting the staff know you value their contributions fosters a positive and supportive work environment.	
7	Having lunch together can facilitate casual conversations among coworkers and foster personal bonds. It could also improve teamwork and communication in a professional setting.	
8	Arranging food-related team activities, such as picnics, happy hours, or meals, allows colleagues to interact outside the workplace and connect in a more relaxed setting.	
9	Establishing spaces where colleagues can gather for meals or snacks fosters social interaction, improves the atmosphere and develops close relationships among team members.	
10	Activities centered around food, such as samosa, phafda, and jalebi parties, can create a happy and positive atmosphere that boosts team morale and could improve overall job satisfaction and output.	
Total Score (out of 10)		

Note:

- Award one point for each "Yes." You are an excellent friend/coworker to everyone else; if your score is higher than 8 points, this implies that you meet all necessary needs and obligations to maintain your friendship and carry out your duties at work.

Maintaining weight loss can be challenging for individuals. It would help if you were mentally prepared for changes and transformations in your social relationships to optimize your results.

Since you've willingly committed to this decision, let's embark on the transformation journey.

Chapter 3

Mastering the Clock: Time Management for a Balanced Life

Many people use the excuse of not having enough time to avoid regular exercise. In today's fast-paced world, people frequently balance multiple responsibilities, including work, family, and social obligations. The pressures of modern life, long work hours, and tight schedules give the impression that exercising is a luxury many cannot afford.

Furthermore, the growth of technology and sedentary occupations might add to feelings of exhaustion and reluctance to engage in physical activity after a long day. The belief that exercises require a significant time commitment, or extensive gym sessions, may also discourage people from implementing more manageable and time-efficient fitness routines into their daily lives.

While time constraints are unavoidable, acknowledging the benefits of physical activity for general well-being and focusing on smaller, regular efforts can help people overcome the "No Time" excuse and make room for a healthy lifestyle.

Time management is vital for maximizing efficiency and productivity. A straight forward time management template is provided for your use. It can be modified to suit your preferences and requirements:

Template for Daily Time Management*: I followed this during my weightloss journey.

Morning:

5:00 a.m. to 7:00 a.m.: Morning routine and awakening.

7:00 a.m. - 7:30 a.m.: Having breakfast.

7:30 a.m. – 8:00 a.m.: Drive to Office

8:00 a.m. to 9:00 a.m.: Task, Top Priority 1

9:00 a.m. to 10:00 a.m.: Midday Priority Task 2.

Between 10:00 a.m. and 11:00 a.m., Task 3

11:00 a.m. - 12:00 p.m.: Task 4

12:00 p.m - 1:00 p.m: Task 5

In the afternoon:

1:00 p.m. to 1:30 p.m.: Having Lunch

1:30 p.m. to 3:00 p.m.: Task 6

3:00 p.m. to 3:30 p.m.: Recharge/Break.

3:30 p.m. - 5:00 p.m.: Evening of Completing Pending Tasks

5:00 p.m. to 6:00 p.m.: Drive back home, close of business.

6:00 p.m. - 7:00 p.m.: Having Dinner.

7:00 p.m. - 8:00 p.m.: Night, Review, and Strategy for the Following Day

8:00 p.m. to 9:00 p.m.: Free time or recreation.

9:00 p.m. to 10:00 p.m.: Routine wind-down.

10:00 p.m.: Bedtime.

Note: This may depend on person to person based on the nature of the profession a person is handling. But it's genuine advice: It's not work controlling you; we manage all our tasks and work. If we initiate the process of change, it will happen. The desire shall come from inside, without any baggage or force.

You may also wonder how many days you must follow such a timetable. In my view, this will act as an agent to change your lifestyle so that it is well integrated into your life. Simply put, your actions must follow discipline to give you a healthy lifestyle throughout your existence.

Remember the following points:

- ✔ Prioritize tasks: Determine and concentrate on the most crucial tasks initially.

- ✔ Time blocking: Allocate specific blocks of time for different activities.

- ✔ Set realistic goals: Ensure that your daily goals are achievable.

- ✔ Minimize interruptions: Disable notifications while engaged in focused work.

- ✔ Rest and breaks: Plan rest and breaks to prevent fatigue and sustain productivity.

- ✔ Examine and modify: Assess your time management regularly, and make necessary adjustments.

Please modify this template to suit your daily schedule, professional obligations or personal inclinations. In addition, consider using digital tools or applications that facilitate enhanced time tracking and management.

Challenges in Time Management

Effective time management can be complex for a variety of reasons. The following are some typical time management difficulties people run into:

- ✔ Delaying: If activities are avoided or delayed, there may be a backlog of work and more tension.

- ✔ Distractions & Interruptions: Distractions at work, continuous notifications, and unforeseen disruptions can all impair concentration and productivity.

- ✔ Absence of Setting Priorities: Identifying and prioritizing crucial tasks can be challenging, which may lead to wasting time on unimportant ones.

- ✔ Overcommitting: Being overburdened and unable to fulfill deadlines might result from taking on too many duties or responsibilities.

- ✔ Poor Planning: Missed deadlines and fast work are consequences of inadequate planning or failing to establish a reasonable schedule.

- ✔ Improbable time estimates: Underestimating the time needed to finish tasks can result in over-commitment and a sense of time pressure.

- ✔ Inability to delegate: Some people need help assigning work, which results in an overwhelming burden and poor time management.

- ✔ Inability to Focus: Failing to focus on a single job can reduce output and increase the time needed to complete tasks.

- ✔ Not Establishing Boundaries: The inability to establish boundaries in one's personal or professional life can lead to non-urgent tasks taking up time.

- ✔ Possible Objectives: Ineffective time management and indecision might result from unclear short- and long-term goals.

- ✔ Perfectionism: Aiming for perfection in every activity could delay and hinder projects from being finished on schedule.

✔ Inaccurate Time Estimation: Inaccurate time estimates might make planning and resource allocation inefficient.

✔ Inability to Learn from Mistakes: Failure to evaluate and modify past time management experiences might cause recurring problems.

✔ Fatigue: Ignoring the need for relaxation and breaks can lead to burnout, which lowers production levels.

✔ Outside Factors: Unexpected circumstances, crises, or shifting priorities can cause timetable disruptions and impact time management.

We often find reasons to justify our inefficiency in managing time. However, for every reason given, there is a potential solution. It's best to focus on solutions and make better use of time.

Moreover, to overcome these obstacles, people must become more self-aware, establish reasonable objectives, prioritize their work, and constantly improve their time management techniques.

Flexibility and willingness to try new things are crucial to determining what works best for one's circumstances.

Chapter 4
Fuel for Life: Crafting a Sustainable Diet Plan

Protein is a necessary macronutrient that is vital to maintaining and promoting several bodily processes. Let's understand why it's required and whether we have a substitute for replacing proteins. Protein's significance extends to several physiological functions and substantially contributes to general health and well-being.

1. The Structure and Function of Cells:

   Proteins are the fundamental units of life. They are the structural foundation of all cells, tissues, and organs. Their presence is essential for maintaining the integrity of cell membranes and promoting intercellular communication. Specialized proteins, known as enzymes, are crucial for catalyzing the biochemical reactions that power cellular functions.

2. Building and Repairing Muscles:

   Proteins are essential for the development and repair of muscles. Muscle tissues experience microtears and strain during exercise. Protein is necessary to produce new proteins, supporting muscle repair and strengthening. Higher protein intake is frequently required for athletes and others who exercise often to sustain muscular growth.

3. Support for the Immune System:

   Proteins make up many components of the immune system, including immune cells and antibodies. Consuming enough protein is essential for creating and maintaining these defense systems. An immune system that is in good working order aids the body in the fight against illnesses and infections, improving general health.

4. Control of Hormones:

   Hormones from proteins control several physiological functions, such as growth, metabolism, and mood. For instance, insulin is a protein hormone essential to glucose metabolism and helps control blood sugar levels. The body's general equilibrium depends on hormonal balance.

5. Activity of Enzyme:

   Specialized proteins called enzymes catalyze biological reactions. They aid in the breakdown of nutrients, guaranteeing that the body absorbs and uses vital elements effectively. Enzymes are essential for bodily functions, such as digestion and food absorption.

6. Control of Weight:

   Protein is essential for both satiety and weight control. Since high-protein foods are typically more satisfying, eating fewer calories is possible. Furthermore, protein requires more digestion energy, increasing the food's thermic effect. A protein-rich diet can help with weight loss and maintenance.

7. Wound Healing and Tissue Repair:

   Proteins play a crucial role in tissue regeneration and repair. The body needs proteins to start mending when it has wounds or injuries. Collagen, a protein in large quantities in connective tissues, is crucial for skin suppleness and wound healing.

8. Keeping pH Balance:

   Specific proteins, which function as buffers, preserve the body's pH equilibrium. Enzymes and other biological reactions require this to work correctly. Keeping pH at its ideal level is essential to avoid disturbing physiological functions.

In conclusion, it is impossible to exaggerate the significance of protein in a human diet. Protein is essential for optimal health because it supports cellular structure and aids in muscle growth, the immune system, and hormone regulation. A well-balanced diet with enough protein prevents nutritional deficiencies and promotes general well-being.

Another vital micronutrient is carbohydrates, which we also call "Carbs". Carbohydrates are necessary for the body to produce energy and support many physiological processes. They are essential since they are the body's primary energy source, impacting mental and physical function and promoting general health and well-being.

1. Source of Energy:

   The body uses carbohydrates as its primary and most effective energy source. It converts carbohydrates into glucose, which cells efficiently use as fuel. This energy drives vital biological processes, such as maintaining body temperature, muscular contractions, and general metabolic processes.

2. Mental Process:

Glucose is the primary energy source that the brain uses extensively. Carbohydrates are a rapid and easy source of glucose for the brain, supporting mental processes such as focus, memory and decision-making. Consuming enough carbohydrates is necessary to keep brain clarity at its best and prevent mental fatigue.

3. Exercise Performance:

Carbohydrates are essential for promoting exercise performance and physical activity. Carbohydrates are a readily available energy source during prolonged or intense physical effort because they are stored as glycogen in the muscles and liver. Maintaining adequate glycogen storage is especially beneficial for athletes as it helps them perform and sustain endurance.

4. Healthy Metabolism:

Consuming the proper kinds and quantities of carbohydrates is essential to maintaining a healthy metabolism. Fruits, vegetables, and whole grains include fiber, a form of carbohydrate that helps with digestion, controls blood sugar, and increases feelings of fullness. Fiber also helps with weight management and helps avoid diseases like type 2 diabetes.

5. Digestive Health:

Dietary fiber is one type of carbohydrate that is essential for maintaining digestive health. Fiber in the stool prevents constipation and makes regular bowel movements easier. It also supports the growth of beneficial gut bacteria, contributing to a healthy and balanced gut microbiome.

6. Absorption of Nutrients:

    Certain nutrients cannot be absorbed without carbohydrates. Carbohydrates improve the small intestine's capacity to absorb calcium, which is essential for bone development and function. Maintaining strong and healthy bones depends on it.

7. Control of Blood Sugar:

    Eating complex carbs, including those found in legumes and healthy grains, aids with blood sugar regulation. Because these carbohydrates break down more slowly, blood glucose is released into the bloodstream gradually. This gradual release lowers the chance of insulin resistance and promotes sustained energy levels, by preventing blood sugar spikes and crashes.

8. Encouraging General Health:

    Carbohydrates provide a balanced diet and supply vital nutrients that improve general health. A vast range of vitamins, minerals, and antioxidants found in fruits, vegetables, and whole grains—high in carbohydrates—support several body processes and aid in preventing chronic diseases.

In summary, carbohydrates are critical to human nutrition because they are an essential energy source for physical and mental tasks. A well-balanced diet, including complex and simple carbs, is crucial to promoting general health, minimizing nutrient shortages and maximizing performance in everyday activities and exercise. When people are aware of the benefits of carbs, they can choose foods that will improve their long-term health and overall well-being.

We have already read about proteins and carbs, and now the next, and last, micronutrient is fats.

Fats, also known as lipids, are crucial in maintaining overall health. Fats have a bad reputation, but they are necessary for many bodily physiological processes. Here is a quick summary of the role that fats play in our health:

1. Source of Energy: Fats are a concentrated source of energy. They offer more than twice as much energy per gram than proteins or carbs. This energy is essential for many biological processes, such as the contraction of muscles, the upkeep of cells, and general metabolic processes.

2. The Structure and Function of Cells: Fats are the basic building blocks of cell membranes. Phospholipid, a lipid that supports cells' structural integrity and fluidity, is essential for the movement of nutrients, cellular communication, and general cell function.

3. Nutrient Absorption: Fats are necessary for the absorption of several vitamins, specifically the fat-soluble vitamins A, D, E, and K. Fats carry these vitamins, making it easier for the digestive system to absorb them. These vitamins are essential for immune system performance, bone health, and antioxidant defense.

4. Production of Hormones: The synthesis of hormones depends on fats. One form of lipid, cholesterol, is used to make steroid hormones like cortisol, estrogen, and testosterone. Growth, metabolism, and the stress response are just a few physiological functions that depend on proper hormone balance.

5. Brain Function: The brain is composed mainly of fats, and dietary fats are crucial for brain health. Omega-3

fatty acids found in certain fish, walnuts, and flaxseeds are essential for cognitive function and may contribute to a reduced risk of neurodegenerative diseases.

6. Insulation and Protection: Body fat, or adipose tissue, acts as an insulator and helps control body temperature. Furthermore, fats buffer internal organs from shocks and injury from the outside world.

7. Inflammation Regulation: Omega-3 fatty acids have anti-inflammatory qualities; they can be found in fatty fish and some plant-based foods. Heart disease and arthritis are only 2 of the health problems associated with chronic inflammation. Consuming these beneficial fats might lessen one's risk of developing associated diseases and control inflammation.

8. Health of Skin and Hair: Essential fatty acids preserve the hydration and elasticity of the skin, which benefits its health. They are also crucial for maintaining healthy nails and hair. A lack of certain fats can lead to brittle hair, dry skin and other dermatological problems.

9. Health of the Heart: Unsaturated fats, mainly monounsaturated and polyunsaturated fats, have been linked to cardiovascular health. A diet high in saturated and trans fats may aggravate heart disease, but they are helpful in lowering risk factors for heart disease and bad cholesterol levels.

10. Weight Regulation: Including good fats in the diet can aid with satiety, which can help with appetite control and calorie restriction. This can prove helpful in preventing obesity and managing weight.

To put it simply, fats are essential for maintaining optimal health. A varied and well-rounded dietary regimen, which, in moderation, incorporates healthy fats, is critical for preventing numerous health issues and maintaining numerous physiological functions. To maximize the advantages of fats while minimizing their drawbacks, it is vital to make informed dietary decisions and to have a comprehensive awareness of the various types of lipids.

Micronutrients, including vitamins and minerals, are essential for preserving general health and well-being. Even though these necessary substances are only needed at trim levels, their lack or insufficiency can cause many health issues. An examination of the significance of vitamins and minerals for human health is provided below:

1. The Role of Cells: Minerals, including calcium, potassium, and salt, are essential for sustaining various cellular processes, enabling cellular communication, and preserving the fluid balance inside and surrounding cells. Similarly, vitamins, such as vitamin C, aid in creating collagen, an essential structural protein in cells.

2. Bone Health: Vitamin D, calcium, phosphorus, and magnesium are essential for the development and maintenance of strong bones. Calcium is a significant part of bone structure, and vitamin D facilitates its absorption. These nutrients are critical for maintaining ideal bone health and preventing osteoporosis-related diseases.

3. Energy Metabolism: B vitamins are essential for energy metabolism. They include B1 (thiamine), B2 (riboflavin), B3 (niacin), B5 (pantothenic acid), B6 (pyridoxine), B7 (biotin), B9 (folate), and B12 (cobalamin). They support the healthy operation of the neurological system, the production of red blood cells, and the conversion of food into energy.

4. Immune System Support: Minerals like zinc and selenium, as well as vitamins A, C, D, and E, support a healthy immune system. These micronutrients play essential roles in immune function, producing antibodies, preserving epidermal integrity, and controlling inflammation.

5. Hemorrhaging and Hemostasis: Vitamin K is necessary for blood coagulation to stop excessive bleeding. It also helps wounds heal by promoting the manufacture of proteins required for tissue repair. Having enough vitamin K is essential for keeping the circulatory system functioning properly.

6. Antioxidant Protection: Together with minerals like manganese and selenium, vitamins C and E are antioxidants. They scavenge free radicals that can damage cells and accelerate aging and chronic illnesses. Antioxidants are essential for preserving overall health and shielding cells from oxidative damage.

7. Eye and Vision Health: Vitamin A is essential for the preservation of eye health and vision. It is a part of the pigment in the retina called rhodopsin, which is necessary for color and low-light perception. Vitamin A deficiency can cause night blindness and other eye problems.

8. Nervous System Function: Vitamins B1, B6, and B12, as well as minerals like potassium and magnesium, are vital for preserving the nervous system's health and functionality. They support neurotransmitter production, neuron signaling and general neurological well-being.

9. Oxygenation and Iron Transport: Hemoglobin, the protein in red blood cells that carries oxygen throughout

the body, depends on iron to function. Sufficient iron consumption is essential to prevent anemia and ensure maximum oxygenation of tissues in the body.

10. Hormone Regulation: Minerals and vitamins play a role in the production and control of hormones. For instance, vitamin D affects hormone balance, and iodine is essential for synthesizing thyroid hormones. Many physiological systems depend on hormones functioning correctly.

In summary, vitamins and minerals are essential for preserving health and avoiding shortages that can result in several diseases. A varied and balanced diet, comprising a wide variety of nutrient-rich foods, is necessary to ensure an appropriate intake of these micronutrients. Knowing their bodily functions emphasizes the importance of making educated food decisions to promote overall well-being.

Chapter 5
Strong Body, Strong Mind: Building an Effective Workout Routine

Before beginning any new fitness regimen, speaking with a healthcare provider is crucial, particularly considering your specific age and medical conditions. Assuming you have the green light for resistance training, here's a sample training program for Males, Females, and Teens. This may vary from person to person and is only for indicative purposes for selected cases, as stated below.

Case 1: Here's a sample 4-day resistance training program for a 45-year-old male weighing 82kg and height 165cm. This schedule allows for proper recovery by focusing on different muscle groups each day:

Day 1: Full Body Workout

- 3 sets of 10 repetitions for squats.
- Bench Press: Three Sets, Ten Reps.
- 3 sets of 12 repetitions for bent-over rows.
- Leg Press: 12 repetitions in 3 sets.
- 3 sets of planks, held for 30 to 60 seconds.

Day 2: Light cardio or rest

Day 3: Push (upper body)

- Overhead Press: 3 sets x 10 reps.

- Dumbbell Flyes: 3 sets x 12 reps.
- Tricep dips: 12 repetitions in 3 sets.
- Hammer curls: 12 reps in 3 sets.
- Russian Twists: 10 reps on each side, 3 sets of 20.

Day 4: Light cardio or rest

Day 5: Lower Body

- Deadlifts: 8 repetitions in 3 sets.
- Lunges: 12 repetitions x 3 sets (per leg)
- Leg curls: 12 repetitions in 3 sets.
- Bench Presses: 3 Sets x 15 Reps.
- Plank: 3 sets, hold for 30-60 seconds.

Day 6: Light cardio or rest

Day 7: Upper Body (Pull)

- Pull-Ups or Lat Pulldowns: 3 sets of 10 repetitions.
- Seated Cable Rows: 3 sets x 12 reps.
- Face Pulls: 3 Sets of 12 Reps.
- Barbell Curl: 12 reps in 3 sets.
- Bicycle Crunches: 3 sets x 20 reps.

Always remember to warm-up before and cool down after your workouts. Also, change the weight and intensity in accordance with your development and degree of fitness. If you're new to exercising or have any concerns, it's always a good idea to speak with a fitness expert to make sure the program is appropriate for your unique needs and goals.

Case 2: 3-day resistance training program for a 45-year-old male weighing 82 kg and height 165 cm. This program targets many muscular areas by combining isolation and complex exercises:

Day 1: Full Body

- Squats: 10 reps in 4 sets.
- Bench Press: 10 repetitions in 4 sets.
- Bent-Over Rows: 4 sets x 12 reps.
- Leg Press: 12 repetitions in 3 sets.
- Plank: 3 sets, hold for 30-60 seconds.

Day 2: Light cardio or rest

Day 3: Upper Body (Push)

- Bench Press: 4 sets of 10 repetitions.
- Dumbbell Flyes: 4 sets x 12 reps.
- Tricep dips: 12 repetitions in 3 sets.
- Hammer curls: 12 reps in 3 sets.
- Russian Twists: 3 sets x 20 reps (10 on each side),
- Face Pulls: 3 Sets of 12 Reps.
- Barbell Curl: 12 reps in 3 sets.

Day 4: Light cardio or rest

Day 5: Lower Body

- Deadlifts: 8 reps in 4 sets.
- Lunges: 12 reps in 4 sets (per leg)
- Leg curls: 12 repetitions in 3 sets.
- Bench Presses: 3 Sets x 15 Reps.
- Plank: 3 sets, hold for 30-60 seconds.

Day 6: Light cardio or rest

Day 7: Light cardio or rest

Always listen to your body and modify the weights according to your fitness level. Always warm-up before starting your workout and cool down afterward. As previously said, it is recommended that you speak with a healthcare provider or fitness expert to make sure the program is appropriate for your particular needs and health issues.

Case 3: 4-day resistance training program designed to help a 45-year-old woman maintain a healthy lifestyle, tone her body, and increase her overall strength. It is always advised to speak with a healthcare provider or fitness expert before beginning a new exercise regimen.

Day 1: Complete Body Strength Warm-Up: 10 minutes of mild aerobic exercise, such as jumping jacks or brisk jogging.

- Stretches that are dynamic for the main muscle groups.
- 3 sets of 12 repetitions for squats.
- Bench Press/Push-Ups: 3 sets of 10 repetitions.
- slouched over, Rows: 3 sets, 12 repetitions.
- Dumbbell lunges: 3 sets, 10 repetitions for each leg.
- 3 sets of planks, held for 30 to 60 seconds.
- Cool-down: Major muscle groups, static stretches

Day 2: Core and Cardio

- Cardio: Run, bike, or use an elliptical for thirty minutes at a moderate effort.
- 3 sets of 20 repetitions for crunches.
- Three sets of 15 reps on each side for Russian twists.
- Leg Raises: Three Sets, 15 Reps
- Plank with Varying Leg Lifts: 12 reps per leg, 3 sets.

Day 3: Active Recuperation, or Rest

- Take up gentle exercises, like yoga or walking, to aid in your recovery.

Day 4: Warm-up for Upper Body Strength: 10 minutes of mild cardio.

- Shoulder stretches and arm circles.

- Bench Press: Three Sets, Ten Reps.

- 3 sets of 12 repetitions for lat pulldowns or pull-ups.

- 3 sets of 12 repetitions for dumbbell chest flies

- Skull Crushers or Tricep Dips: 3 sets of 12 repetitions.

- Shoulder taps and plank: 3 sets of 15 repetitions on each side.

- Lower body stretches as a cool-down.

Day 5: Strengthening of the Lower Body

Warm-up: 10 minutes of gentle aerobic exercise.

- Hip stretches and leg swings

- Strengthening Exercise:

- Deadlifts: 3 sets, 10 repetitions.

- Leg Press: Three Sets, 12 Reps.

- Leg Curls While Seated: 3 Sets, 12 Reps

- 3 sets of 15 repetitions for calf raises.

- Three sets of 15 reps each for the plank with hip dips.

- Cooling down: Lower body stretches.

Days 6-7: Active Recuperation or Rest

- Take a nap, or do gentle recovery exercises like yoga or walking.

Observations:

- ✔ Advancement: As your strength increases, gradually increase the weights or resistance.

- ✔ Form Is Essential: Pay attention to form to avoid injury.

- ✔ Pay Attention to Your Body: If you experience more than your usual muscle soreness, consider reducing the intensity or seek a consultation from a fitness expert.

- ✔ Hydration: Throughout your exercise, drink plenty of water.

You can modify the program to suit your fitness level and preferences. Maintaining consistency is essential; resistance training should be combined with a good diet, and other lifestyle practices.

Case 4: A 3-day fitness schedule for a 21-year-old female who weighs 65 kg and is 152.4 cm tall.

Strength, flexibility and cardiovascular fitness exercises are necessary for a slender body. Adjusting the exercise schedule based on each person's preferences and fitness level is critical. This is an example of a fitness schedule for a woman who wants to get in shape:

Day 1: Whole-body strength training and cardio

The warm-up is 10 minutes of gentle exercise, such as jogging in place or doing jumping jacks.

- Cardio: 20 to 30 minutes of moderate-intensity physical activity (brisk walking, cycling, or jogging).

Strengthening Exercise:

- 3 sets of 15 repetitions of bodyweight squats.
- Three sets of 12 reps for push-ups or modified push-ups.

- Bent-over rows: 3 sets of 12 repetitions with light dumbbells or tension bands.
- Plank: 3 sets, each lasting 30 to 60 seconds.

Day 2: Rest or Active Recuperation

- Take gentle exercises like yoga, stretching, or walking to aid healing.

Day 3: Light aerobics for 10 minutes to warm-up the core

- Cardio: 20–30 minutes of high-intensity interval training (HIIT), such as intervals of cycling or sprinting.

Fundamental Exercises:

- 3 sets of 20 repetitions for crunches.
- Russian twists, 3 sets of 15 reps on each side
- Leg Raises: Three Sets, 15 Reps
- Plank: 3 sets, holding each for 30 to 60 seconds.

Day 4: Rest or Active Recovery

- Take it easy and concentrate on getting better.

Day 5: Lower Body Strength Training and Cardio.

- Warm-up: 10 minutes of gentle aerobic exercise.
- Cardio: 20 to 30 minutes at a moderate heart rate.

Strength Training for the Lower Body:

- Lunges: 12 repetitions per leg, 3 sets.
- Step-ups: 3 sets of 15 repetitions per leg, using a bench or step.
- 3 sets of 15 repetitions for glute bridges.
- Plank: 3 sets, each lasting 30 to 60 seconds.

Day 6: Stretching or Yoga

- Concentrate on your flexibility and relaxation with a yoga class or a focused stretching regimen.

Day 7: Leisure or Mild Exercise

- Take a day off work, or go for a stroll, or bike ride.

Observations:

- ✔ Advancement: As your fitness level rises, progressively raise the intensity and difficulty of your workouts.

- ✔ Consistency: Try to work out at least 3 to 4 days a week.

- ✔ Pay attention to your body. If you feel pain or discomfort, adjust your activities or seek advice from a fitness expert.

- ✔ Hydration: To stay hydrated, sip lots of water throughout the day.

Before beginning a new workout regimen, get advice from a healthcare or fitness professional, particularly if you have any pre-existing medical concerns. Adapt the exercise schedule to your own needs and level of fitness.

Case 5: Provide a training schedule for a man who is 20 years old, weighs 60 kg and is 159 cm tall.

Combining cardiovascular, strength, and focused abdominal workouts is a thorough workout strategy for developing six-pack abs. Because it is impossible to lose fat from just one area of the body, complete body fat reduction is necessary to achieve visible abs. This is an example exercise schedule:

Day 1: Complete Body Strength Training

- The warm-up is 10 minutes of gentle exercise, such as jogging in place or doing jumping jacks.

Strengthening Exercise:

- 3 sets of 10–12 repetitions for squats.
- 3 sets of 10–12 repetitions for deadlifts.
- 3 sets of 10–12 repetitions for the bench press or push-ups.
- slouched over, Rows: 3 sets, 10–12 repetitions
- Plank: 3 sets, each lasting 30 to 60 seconds.
- Cardio: 20 to 30 minutes of moderate-intensity physical activity (brisk walking, cycling, or jogging).

Day 2: Light aerobics for 10 minutes to warm-up the core.

- Cardio: 20–30 minutes of high-intensity interval training (HIIT), such as intervals of cycling or sprinting.

Fundamental Exercises:

- 3 sets of 20 repetitions for Cycle crunches.
- 3 sets of 15 repetitions on each side for Russian twists.
- Leg Raises: Three Sets, 15 Reps
- Plank: 3 sets, each lasting 30 to 60 seconds.

Day 3: Rest or Active Recuperation

- Take gentle exercises like yoga, stretching, or walking to aid healing.

Day 4: Complete Body Strengthening

- Replicate the Day 1 strength training regimen.

Day 5: Core and Cardio

- Replicate the Day 2 cardio and core routines.

Day 6: Rest or Active Recuperation

- Take it easy, relax, and concentrate on getting better.

Day 7: Focus on the Abdomen

- Warm-up: 10 minutes of gentle aerobic exercise.

- HIIT: Do HIIT for 20 to 30 minutes, incorporating movements for the entire body.

Exercises for the Abdomen:

- Three sets of thirty seconds each for plank variations (side planks, planks with leg raises).

- Dangling Leg Raises: Three Sets, 12 Reps.

- Alpinists: Three sets of 20 repetitions.

Observations:

- ✔ Progression: To test your muscles, gradually increase the weights and intensity of your strength training sessions.

- ✔ Consistency: Follow the plan and work out 3 to 4 days a week.

- ✔ Nutrition: Combine the exercise program with a well-balanced diet to promote muscle building and fat reduction.

- ✔ Hydration: To stay hydrated, sip lots of water throughout the day.

To guarantee perfect form and technique, modify the workout plan according to your fitness level, and consider speaking with a fitness professional. Pay attention to your body and adjust as necessary.

Case 6: 7-day training schedule to improve the height of a 12-year-old child, who weighs 40 kg and measures 140 cm tall.

It's crucial to remember that height is influenced by genetics. While exercise can improve overall health and well-being, no workout program can guarantee an increase in height.

A well-rounded exercise routine, including yoga, can help a child's posture, flexibility and mental attention. Here's a simple, kid-friendly yoga program:

Day 1: Cardiovascular Exercise

- Jump jacks: 3 sets of one minute.
- Run or jog in place for 10 minutes.
- Cycling: 15 minutes.

Day 2: Strength Training

- Bodyweight exercises (push-ups, squats, lunges): 3 sets of 10-15 repetitions.
- To do Tadasana, stand tall with feet together and arms by your sides. Reach your arms up, palms facing each other.

Day 3: Flexibility and Stretching

- Yoga or Pilates (Surya Namaskar) is a 20-30 minute yoga practice.
- Vrikshasana: 10-15 minutes

Day 4: Cardiovascular Exercise

- Swim for 20 minutes.
- Skipping rope for 10 minutes.
- Dancing for 20 minutes.

Day 5: Active Play

- Participate in sports such as football, tennis, or your favorite sport for 30–45 minutes.

Day 6: Strength Training

- Bodyweight exercises: Three sets of 10-15 repetitions.
- Planks or Push-up! Extra challenge: 3 sets of 10 to twelve reps.

Day 7: Rest and Recreation

- Allow for rest and healing. Encourage recreational activities, such as walking, hiking, and cycling.

Ensure the youngster is supervised during strength training activities to maintain good form and avoid injury. Emphasize the need for adequate nutrition, including a well-balanced diet rich in vitamins and minerals, for healthy growth and development.

Contact a healthcare practitioner or a certified fitness trainer before beginning any workout program, especially for youngsters. Certified trainers can provide tailored advice depending on the child's requirements and health state. Encourage deep, deliberate breathing throughout each pose. Make the session fun and engaging, tailoring the positions to the child's comfort and skills.

Always prioritize safety, and if you have any health issues, speak with a healthcare practitioner or a certified yoga guru before beginning a yoga program.

Chapter 6

Calm in Chaos: Proven Stress Management Techniques

Stress, also called a stressor, is the body's and mind's reaction to a perceived threat or demand. It's the body's method of responding to an imagined or actual circumstance that calls for action. Stress sets off a complicated series of events known as the "fight or flight" reaction, which causes the body to alter physiologically and release hormones to prepare to respond to the perceived threat.

Essential elements of stress consist of the following:

Stressors:

- These are the events or triggers that set off the stress reaction. Stressors can be internal, like self-imposed demands or fears, or external, such as work pressure, money troubles, or relationship issues.

  - ✔ Physiological Response: In response to stress, the body releases hormones that prime the body for action, such as cortisol and adrenaline. This response entails changes in heart rate, blood pressure, and the level of attention to respond to the perceived threat.

  - ✔ Cognitive and Emotional Reaction: Stress often leads to changes in thoughts and emotions, resulting in feelings of overwhelm, fear, worry, or anxiety. It also affects cognitive processes, such as memory and focus.

✔ Behavioral Reaction: Individuals may exhibit behaviors in response to stress. While some people could become more restless or agitated, others might become more engaged and vigilant. Reactions to stress in behavior differ significantly.

There are various kinds of stress:

- Acute Stress: This type of stress is usually strong and occurs briefly. Specific situations or events can trigger it, and it typically disappears once the stressor is removed, or the problem is resolved.

- Chronic Stress: Persistent stress lasts a long time and may result from persistent problems, including chronic health ailments like Alzheimer's Disease, Dementias, Arthritis, Asthma, Other Inflammatory Bowel Diseases, Irritable Bowel Syndrome, etc., financial difficulties, or work-related stress.

- Eustress: This type of stress is constructive and is linked to drive, enthusiasm, and a feeling of achievement. Stress can result from difficult but controllable circumstances, such as beginning a new work or a fulfilling project.

- Distress: Often linked to emotions of worry, annoyance, or overload, distress is the negative form of stress. Difficult situations or persistent problems might bring on a stressful existence.

It's crucial to remember that not all stress has adverse effects. In the short-term, stress can be a healthy, adaptive reaction that helps people overcome obstacles and deal with life-threatening situations.

Long-term stress that isn't adequately managed might harm one's physical and emotional well-being. General well-being requires stress management through the adoption of a healthy lifestyle, the practice of relaxation techniques, and seeking assistance when necessary.

Effects of stress on a person's life?

Stress is a normal reaction to difficult circumstances or imagined dangers, and it can have a significant impact on a person's life.

While occasional stress can be a natural part of life, prolonged or extreme stress can negatively affect many facets of a person's health and well-being.

The following are a few possible effects of stress on human life:

- Physical Health:

  ✔ Weakened Immune System: Long-term stress can undermine an individual's immune system, leaving them more vulnerable to disease.

  ✔ Long-term stress is associated with high blood pressure, heart disease and other cardiovascular issues.

  ✔ Stress can impact digestion, resulting in problems like indigestion, stomach pain or irritable bowel syndrome (IBS).

- Mental Health:

  ✔ Depression and Anxiety: Prolonged stress is associated with a higher risk of depression and anxiety.

  ✔ Sleep Disorders: Insomnia and other sleep disorders can result from stress disrupting sleep cycles.

- Cognitive Function:

  ✔ Extended stress can harm one's ability to concentrate, remember things and make decisions.

- Emotional Well-Being:

  ✔ Mood Swings: Stress can intensify irritation, mood swings and an overall feeling of unease.

  ✔ Diminished Happiness: Prolonged stress can make it harder to feel content and joyful daily.

- Behavioral Shifts:

  ✔ Unhealthy Coping Strategies: When under stress, people may turn to unhealthy coping strategies, including binge eating, drug usage, or smoking.

  ✔ Social retreat: Stress can cause strained friendships, and family ties, as well as social retreat.

- Work Performance:

  ✔ Reduced Productivity: Prolonged stress can affect one's ability to perform at work, resulting in lower output, focusing, and increased absenteeism.

  ✔ Burnout is a state of physical and emotional tiredness caused by extended stress at work.

- Sexual and Reproductive Health:

  ✔ Menstrual irregularities: Women who experience stress may experience irregular periods.

  ✔ Problems with Fertility: Prolonged stress has been linked to infertility in both men and women.

- Higher Chance of Chronic Illnesses:

  ✔ Type 2 Diabetes: There is a link between long-term stress and a higher chance of type 2 diabetes.

  ✔ Inflammation: A correlation exists between chronic inflammation and various disorders, with stress potentially intensifying the condition.

It's crucial to remember that everyone experiences stress differently and that they may also employ various coping strategies. Reducing stress's detrimental impacts on general well-being can be achieved mainly by managing it with good lifestyle choices, relaxing methods, and getting help when needed.

It is essential to seek professional assistance from a healthcare physician or mental health expert if stress becomes unbearable.

Part of our body that experiences the most stress?

Stress can have a wide range of effects on different bodily regions. The following are some bodily systems and particular organs that are especially vulnerable to the harmful consequences of long-term stress:

- Effects on the Cardiovascular System: Prolonged stress may raise the chance of developing cardiovascular problems. Elevated blood pressure, atherosclerosis (artery narrowing), and a higher risk of heart disease are possible outcomes.

- Effects on the Immune System: Extended stress can weaken the body's defenses against infections and diseases, explaining why people who regularly experience stress may get sick more frequently.

- Effects on the Digestive System: Stress can impact the digestive system, causing problems such as acid reflux, indigestion, IBS, and inflammatory bowel illnesses (such as ulcerative colitis or Crohn's disease).

- Effects on the Endocrine System: Stress can impact the hormone-producing glands that make up the endocrine system. Hormone imbalances brought on by prolonged stress can cause adrenal fatigue, irregular menstruation, and other problems.

- Central Nervous System (CNS): Both the brain and the CNS are affected by stress. It may impact mental processes like memory, focus, and judgment. A higher risk of anxiety and depression is also associated with chronic stress.

- Effects on the Musculoskeletal System: Stress can aggravate temporomandibular joint (TMJ) abnormalities and induce muscle strain and migraines. Muscle tension and back discomfort are 2 conditions that can experience escalation due to chronic muscle strain.

- Effects on the Reproductive System: Stress affects reproductive health. It may impact fertility and cause irregular menstruation in women. Prolonged stress in men might affect sperm production and testosterone levels.

- Effects on the Respiratory System: Stress can cause respiratory diseases such as asthma or chronic obstructive pulmonary disease (COPD). It can also cause someone to breathe shallowly or too much.

The key to reducing stress's detrimental effects on general health is to manage it with appropriate coping mechanisms, including regular exercise, relaxation techniques, enough sleep, and seeking support when needed. If stress becomes too much, it's best to get expert assistance from medical or mental health professionals.

How can stress be released?

Changing one's lifestyle and implementing good coping strategies are essential to managing and reducing stress. The following are a few techniques that could reduce stress:

- Frequent Workout:

    ✔ Take up a regular exercise routine, such as yoga, jogging, walking, or swimming. Engaging in physical activity helps release stored tension and triggers the release of endorphins, natural mood enhancers.

- Techniques for Deep Breathing and Relaxation:

  - ✔ Engage in progressive muscular relaxation, meditation, or deep breathing exercises. These methods can help lower stress levels and calm the neurological system.

  - ✔ Sufficient Sleep: Get a good night's rest. Sleep deprivation can aggravate stress and make it harder to handle problems. Create a cozy sleeping environment and stick to a regular sleep schedule.

- Optimal Nutrition:

  - ✔ Consume a varied diet rich in well-balanced nutrients. Avoid processed snacks, sugary meals, and excessive caffeine as they might worsen mood swings and energy changes.

  - ✔ Time management tips include setting realistic objectives prioritizing work and efficiently managing time. Enlarging projects into smaller, more doable steps can help them feel less.

- Social Support: Contact loved ones, close friends, or a support system. Speaking with a trusted person about your emotions might offer perspective and emotional support.

- Awareness and Mind-Body Techniques: Exercise mindfulness and participate in tai chi, yoga, or meditation. These techniques can lessen the effects of stress and maintain present-moment awareness.

- Restrict Stimulants: Limit your consumption of stimulants like nicotine and coffee, especially in the hours before bed.

- Hobbies and Leisure Activities: Engage in things you enjoy to decompress and unwind. Engaging in hobbies and leisure activities can relieve stress and give one a feeling of achievement.

- Establishing Boundaries: To prevent taking on too many duties, learn when to say "NO" and establish reasonable boundaries. Make self-care a priority and schedule downtime.

- Professional Support: If stress becomes too much to handle on your own, you should consider getting professional help from a therapist, counselor, or mental health specialist.

- Positive Thinking: Refute pessimistic ideas and engage in constructive thought. Instead of concentrating on issues, pay attention to solutions.

Understanding that stress management is a customized process and that what works for one person might not work for another is crucial. Try out various tactics to determine which combo works best for you.

If stress substantially influences your life, seeking help from a healthcare professional or mental health specialist is essential. They can offer you individualized guidance and assistance based on your circumstances.

Now, let's see the effects of stress on people's sexual lives.

Stress can affect a person's sex life in several ways, including both the psychological and physical elements. Here are a few ways that stress may affect one's sexual orientation:

- Sexual Drive (Libido):

  ✔ Prolonged stress can lower libido due to elevated stress hormones, leading to reduced sexual desire.

  ✔ It can cause erectile dysfunction in men and vaginal dryness in women, affecting physical arousal and comfort.

  ✔ Stress can create emotional barriers, reducing intimacy and connection between partners.

- Relationship Dynamics:

  ✔ Stress can increase tension and conflict, disrupting sexual satisfaction.

  ✔ Hormonal imbalances caused by stress can impact sexual desire and function.

  ✔ Anxiety and depression, often linked to stress, can further diminish sexual desire.

- Lifestyle Factors:

  ✔ Stress may lead to unhealthy coping behaviors like overeating, smoking, or excessive alcohol use, all of which can harm sexual health.

  ✔ Exhaustion from stress can reduce energy and motivation for sexual activity.

- Fertility Issues:

  ✔ Stress can worsen fertility problems, affecting women's menstrual cycles and reproductive hormones, making conception more difficult.

Prioritizing general well-being and implementing stress management techniques are necessary to address stress and its effects on sexual health.

Here are some strategies to lessen the adverse effects of stress on a sexual life:

  ✔ Communication: Discuss tensions and worries with a spouse openly and sincerely.

✔ Practices for Reducing Stress: Take part in stress-relieving, mindfulness, and relaxation exercises.

✔ Professional Support: Consulting with therapists or counselors to help manage stress or resolve relationship problems.

✔ Maintaining a healthy lifestyle entail getting enough sleep, eating balanced food, and exercising frequently.

It is essential to seek help from healthcare professionals or sexual health experts for a complete examination and suitable interventions if stress-related sexual issues continue or significantly impact one's well-being.

Let's take the case of the effects of stress on a student's life.

Stress can significantly impact students' lives and harm their well-being, mental health, and academic achievement. Students might experience stress from various factors, such as social pressures, financial worries, academic pressures, and uncertainty about the future.

The following are some effects that stress may have on students:

- Academic Achievement:

    ✔ Impaired Concentration: Prolonged stress can make it difficult for a person to focus and remember information, which makes it harder for kids to concentrate on their academics.

    ✔ Reduced Memory Function: Stress can cause memory problems, making it difficult for kids to remember the material when taking tests or doing homework.

    ✔ Mental Health: Anxiety and despair. Social pressures, in addition to academic stress, can cause or intensify anxiety and hopelessness in students.

- ✔ Increased susceptibility to Mental Health Disorders: Students' general psychological well-being may be impacted by prolonged stress, which may raise their chances of acquiring mental health disorders.

- Physical Health:

  - ✔ Sleep Disturbances: Stress can cause sleep disorders, including insomnia or erratic sleep patterns, which can be detrimental to one's mental and physical well-being.

  - ✔ Headaches and Physical Tension: Students may suffer from tension headaches, muscle aches, and other stress-related problems.

- Social Relationships:

  - ✔ Withdrawal and Isolation: Stress can intensify emotions of withdrawal in students, which makes them avoid social situations and activities.

  - ✔ Relationship Conflict: Academic stress may negatively impact peer, friend, and family relationships, leading to arguments and tense exchanges.

- Coping Strategies:

  - ✔ Unhealthy Coping Strategies: When under stress, students may turn to unhealthy coping strategies, including substance misuse, overindulgence in food, or excessive use of electronics.

- Future Concerns:

  - ✔ Employment and Future Anxiety: Stress can result from worries about future employment opportunities and uncertainty when students approach graduation or make significant academic decisions.

- Financial Strains:

  ✔ Financial Stress: Students struggling to pay for their education, living expenses, or student loans, may feel more stressed than usual.

- Managing Time:

  ✔ The Need to Meet Deadlines: The pressure to meet deadlines for courses, papers, and exams can lead to time management difficulties and increased stress levels.

- Academic Burnout:

  ✔ Academic burnout, marked by emotional tiredness, decreased motivation, and a deterioration in academic performance, can be caused by prolonged stress without appropriate coping methods.

Children must understand the warning signals of stress and use healthy coping mechanisms.

Among the methods used by students to reduce stress are the following:

✔ Time management tips include setting priorities, making reasonable timetables, and dividing work into digestible chunks.

✔ A healthy lifestyle consists of getting enough sleep, eating a balanced diet, and exercising frequently.

✔ Social Support: To talk about difficulties and express worries, get help from friends, family, or counseling services.

✔ Strict "NO" to mobiles or pads as this will not let you focus on your studies.

✔ Techniques for Mindfulness and Relaxation: To lower stress levels, engage in deep breathing exercises, mindfulness, or meditation.

✔ Professional Assistance: If stress worsens, seek advice from student counseling programs or mental health specialists.

✔ Educational establishments can also help by providing resources for stress management, fostering a supportive environment, and raising students' understanding of mental health issues.

The following are the best methods to reduce stress.

Adopting appropriate coping strategies and lifestyle habits is essential to managing and lowering stress. Here are a few practical strategies for reducing anxiety:

✔ Frequent Exercise: Regularly participate in physical activities, such as cycling, walking, running, or jogging. Exercise releases natural mood enhancers called endorphins.

✔ Techniques for Deep Breathing and Relaxation: To soothe the nervous system and lower stress levels, engage in progressive muscle relaxation, meditation, or deep breathing techniques.

✔ Sufficient Sleep: Get a good night's rest, create a cozy sleeping environment, and stick to a regular sleep schedule.

✔ Eating Healthily: Make sure your food is well-balanced and contains different nutrients. Avoid processed snacks, sugary meals and too much caffeine.

✔ Time management tips include setting reasonable objectives, prioritizing work, and dividing more complex jobs into minor, more doable activities. Good time management can lessen feelings of overwhelm.

✔ Social Support: Contact loved ones, close friends, or a support system. You can also get emotional support by talking to someone you trust about your feelings and worries.

✔ Meditation and mindfulness: To remain in the present moment, practice mindfulness. Mindful practices, like yoga and meditation, can also help you relax and reduce stress.

✔ Hobbies and Leisure Activities: Take part in enjoyable activities that make you feel good about yourself. Recreational pursuits and hobbies offer a healthy way to decompress.

✔ Limit Stimulants: Cut back on your consumption of stimulants, such as nicotine and caffeine, particularly in the hours before bed.

✔ Positive Thought: Discard pessimistic ideas and concentrate on the good things happening. Keeping an optimistic mindset might help lower stress.

✔ Realistic Expectations: Make sure your expectations and goals are reasonable for yourself. Steer clear of creating unrealistic expectations that could cause needless tension.

✔ Acquire the Ability to Say No: Know your boundaries and don't be afraid to refuse requests when necessary. Taking on an excessive amount of work can make you stressed.

✔ Journaling: Record your feelings and ideas in a written diary. This can help you gain perspective, recognize stressors, and investigate possible fixes.

- ✔ Expert Assistance: Seek professional assistance from therapists, counselors, or mental health specialists if stress becomes unbearable or chronic.

- ✔ Spend time in the great outdoors and breathe in some fresh air. Research has shown that engaging in outdoor activities and natural settings reduces stress.

Remember that different tactics fit different people, so you should experiment until you find the one that works best for you. Long-term efficacy in stress management techniques depends on consistently incorporating them into your daily routine. Seeking advice from a medical practitioner or mental health specialist is advised if stress continues or gets worse.

Chapter 7

The Art of Rest: Unlocking the Benefits of Quality Sleep

1, 6 Globally, 62% of individuals claim they need to receive the recommended minimum of 7 hours of sleep each night (Golombék D. A. et al, 2023) (Phillips Global Sleep Survey, 2019). 4 The testosterone level of a man who sleeps 4 to 5 hours a night is comparable to that of a man 10 years his senior. In other words, sleep deprivation ages a man by 10 years in terms of essential aspects of well-being, and equivalently, it also negatively impacts the reproductive system in women (M Walker, 2017).

Sleep is essential. You cannot function or survive without it. When your body is at rest, your brain works, establishing all the communication between nerve cells or neurons. While you sleep, the day's activities are arranged by neurons in your nerve cells and stored in Memory for easy retrieval. According to recent research, it also cleans, clearing your brain of any toxins that accumulate while awake. Your brain detoxes itself more efficiently the deeper you sleep. Adults usually require 7-9 hours of sleep for optimal brain function, yet many do not get it.

The process of sleep is dynamic and complex. Nearly every person on earth experiences a condition of unconsciousness and paralysis, but what exactly is going on inside our bodies when we drift off, and what are the consequences of not getting enough sleep?

5 During sleep, various brain regions are active (NIH, Public Education, 2023).

1. The **hypothalamus** is a small peanut-sized region on the side of our brain. It contains a cluster of nerve cells that control our sleep and awakening. Within the hypothalamus is a space known as the suprachiasmatic nucleus (SCN), a collection of thousands of nerve cells that receive direct exposure to light from our eyesight and control our behaviors.

2. The **brain stem** includes the structures called the pons, medulla, and midbrain, located at the base of the brain. It communicates with the hypothalamus to control sleep and wakefulness. Chemicals such as GABA are produced by sleep-promoting cells in the brain stem and hypothalamus to lower arousal activity. During REM sleep, the brain stem parts, such as the pons and medulla, send signals to relax the muscles for limb movement and body posture. This prevents us from acting out in our dreams.

3. **The Thalamus** is a channel of information sensed by the cerebral cortex, which is part of the brain and is responsible for processing, interpreting, and storing memories from short-term to long-term. During sleep, the Thalamus is quiet and cuts you out from the external world, whereas in REM sleep, it is active and helps send cortex images, sensations, and sounds to form dreams.

4. **The pineal gland** receives the signal from the SCN to increase the production of a hormone called melatonin, which makes you sleep when the light goes off. The pineal gland is present between the 2 hemispheres of the brain.

5. The **basal forebrain** promotes sleep and wakefulness, while the brain acts as an arousal system. It is located between the front and back of the brain. Hormones such as adenosine released from the cells in the forebrain and other body parts help with sleep. Caffeine blocks the adenosine and counteracts sleepiness.

6. The **amygdala** is an almond-shaped structure active during REM sleep and helps process emotions.

Our brain is so powerful that it controls and regulates sleep according to your circadian rhythm.

Throughout the night, our body cycles through 4 distinct stages of sleep, repeating these stages 4 to 5 times. These stages, known as non-REM and REM sleep, each serve a unique purpose in maintaining our overall health and well-being (NIH. Public Education, 2023).

1. During **Stage 1** non-REM sleep, the body transitions from being awake to asleep. This stage is characterized by slow breathing, heart rate, and eye movements, and lasts only a few minutes. The muscles also relax, with occasional twitches, while brain waves commence to slow down from their daytime patterns.

2. During **Stage 2** non-REM sleep, the body transitions from light to deeper sleep. Breathing and heart rate gradually slow down, muscles ease out further, and body temperature drops. Eye movements stop, and brain wave activity reduces, punctuated by brief surges of electrical activity. During repeated sleep cycles, more time is spent in Stage 2 than in previous sleep stages.

3. During **Stage 3**, non-REM Sleep is a deep sleep that refreshes us when we wake up. It is one of the more

extended periods of Sleep that occurs during the early part of the night. During this stage, your breathing and heart rate go at minimum levels, and muscles become so relaxed that waking up may be challenging. Brain wave activity reduces even further.

4. Within 90 minutes of falling asleep, REM sleep starts. During this stage, the eyes move rapidly, going back and forth behind closed lids, and brain wave activity becomes similar to being awake. Heart rate and blood pressure increase to near-waking levels, and breathing becomes faster and more uneven. Most dreaming occurs during REM sleep, although some occur during non-REM sleep.[2] During dreaming, the body temporarily gets paralyzed in the arms and legs to prevent us from acting out our dreams (James W. Kalat, 2016).

The building of memories requires both REM and non-REM sleep.

Imagine a treatment that could improve the immune system, protect the cardiovascular system, aid in weight loss and metabolic management, regulate brain waste clearance, improve productivity, and enhance mood and emotional self-regulation, among other benefits. ***Well, we already have it: Sleep***. (Golombék, D. A., et al, 2023)

But the question is, how to get "sound sleep." You can improve your sleep quality by avoiding caffeine, nicotine, and alcohol before bed, exercising 20-30 minutes a day, but not before going to bed, creating a comfortable, cold and dark room environment, avoiding bright light and loud sounds in the bedroom, and taking a warm bath before going to bed.

So, invest in your sleep to have a rich and healthy life.

References:

1. Golombék, D. A., Booi, L., Campbell, D., Dawson, W. D., Eyre, H. A., Lawlor, B., & Ibáñez, A. (2023). Sleep diplomacy: An approach to boosting global brain health. The Lancet Healthy Longevity. https://doi.org/10.1016/s2666-7568(23)00109-5

2. James W. Kalat, 2016. Biological psychology (Twelfth edition), 273-277, https://www.vlebooks.com/Product/Index/1094464?page=0&startBookmarkId=-1

3. Lewis LD, 2021. *The interconnected causes and consequences of Sleep in the Brain. SCIENCE*; 374:564-68 https://www.science.org/doi/10.1126/science.abi8375

4. M Walker, 2017. *Why We Sleep: Unlocking the Power of Sleep and Dreams.*

5. NIH. Public Education, 2023. *Brain Basics-Understanding Sleep.*

6. https://www.ninds.nih.gov/health-information/public-education/brain-basics/brain-basics-understanding-sleep?search-term=Brain%20Basic%3A

7. Phillips Global Sleep Survey, 2019. *The global pursuit of better Sleep.* https://www.usa.philips.com/c-dam/b2c/master/experience/smartsleep/world-sleep-day/2019/2019-philips-world-sleep-day-survey-results.pdf

Why is Sleep Essential?

Numerous physiological, mental, and emotional processes require sleep. Its multiple roles demonstrate how important it is to general health and well-being. Critical arguments for the need for sleep are as follows:

1. Physical Restoration: The body heals and regenerates during sleep. Deep sleep is when tissues and organs

grow, mend, and maintain themselves. Growth hormone, which is necessary for physical development and maintenance, is released throughout this process.

2. Energy Conservation: Sleep contributes to energy conservation by lowering the metabolic rate and total energy consumption. This enables the body to reallocate energy to vital functions, including tissue growth and repair.

3. Immune Function: A strong immune system depends on getting enough sleep. While you sleep, your immune system creates and releases cytokines, proteins essential to the immunological response. This supports the body's defences against diseases and infections.

4. Memory Consolidation: Learning and memory consolidation depend on sleep. Information learned when awake is organized and processed by the brain, moving it from short-term to long-term memory. This helps with cognitive processes like learning and solving problems.

5. Emotional Well-Being: Getting enough sleep is essential for maintaining psychological and emotional stability. It improves emotional resilience, lowers irritation, and stabilizes mood. A prolonged lack of sleep is connected to a higher risk of mood disorders like anxiety and sadness.

6. Cognitive Function: The ability to pay attention, concentrate, and make decisions depends on getting enough sleep. Having a restful night's sleep improves one's ability to think, solve problems, and maintain general mental clarity.

7. Hormonal Regulation: Sleep affects the balance of hormones linked to stress, hunger, and growth.

Sleep-related hormonal control plays a role in maintaining general hormonal balance and health.

8. Regulation of Metabolism: Sleep influences insulin sensitivity and glucose metabolism. Long-term sleep deprivation has been linked to a higher risk of metabolic diseases such as diabetes and obesity.

9. Cardiovascular Health: Getting enough Sleep is associated with improved cardiovascular health. Sleep supports general cardiovascular health, lowers inflammation, and controls blood pressure. Long-term sleep deprivation is linked to a higher risk of heart disease and stroke.

10. Physical Performance: Those who participate in physical activity, such as athletes, benefit from getting enough sleep. It enhances general physical performance, coordination and muscle recovery.

11. Safety: Sleep is essential for maintaining awareness and quick reflexes. Sleep deprivation can affect cognitive abilities, raising the possibility of mishaps and mistakes.

12. Longevity: Research has linked getting enough sleep to a longer and healthier life. Prolonged sleep deprivation is associated with a higher risk of death.

Sleep is essential to life, promoting mental clarity, physical health, and efficient operation. To support general health and vigor, it is imperative to establish effective sleep hygiene habits and guarantee adequate, high-quality sleep.

How can we sleep soundly like a baby?

It's well known that babies can sleep soundly and profoundly. Although it may not be possible for adults to mimic a baby's sleep patterns fully, several techniques and good sleep hygiene habits can enhance sleep quality and encourage a more peaceful night.

Here are some pointers for getting a good night's sleep, just like a baby:

- Create a Regular Sleep Schedule: Stick to a normal sleep routine by going to bed and waking up at the exact times each day, even on the weekends. Consistency regulates the body's internal clock.

- Establish a Calm Bedtime Schedule: Create a relaxing nighttime ritual to let your body know when to relax. This could involve taking a warm bath, reading a book, or practicing yoga.

- Establish a Comfortable Sleep Environment: Make sure your bedroom is restful. This involves a cozy mattress and pillows, and a quiet, dark, cold atmosphere. Consider putting away light-emitting electronics and using blackout curtains.

- Limit Your Screen Time Before Bed: At least one hour before bed, limit your time spent in front of screens, including computers, TVs, phones, and tablets. The blue light that screens emit may inhibit the hormone melatonin, which promotes sleep.

- Control Your Anxiety and Stress: Before going to bed, try practicing stress-reduction methods, like deep breathing exercises, mindfulness, or meditation, to help clear your head and lessen worry.

- Restrict Stimulants: Refrain from using stimulants, such as nicotine and caffeine, right before bed. Certain drugs may make it difficult to fall asleep.

- Exercise Frequently, but try to wrap it up a few hours before bed. Frequent exercise helps improve sleep quality, but vigorous exercise right before bed may have the opposite impact.

- Keep an Eye on Your Diet: Pay attention to what you eat after dark. Be wary of large, spicy meals and snacks right before bed as they can make you uncomfortable and interfere with sleep.

- Expose Yourself to Natural Light: To obtain exposure to natural light, spend some time outside during the day. Natural light supports a healthy sleep-wake cycle and aids in circadian rhythm regulation in the body.

- Limit Naps: If you take naps during the day, limit the length to 20 to 30 minutes and avoid naps right before bed.

- Remain Hydrated: To reduce interruptions from late-night toilet breaks, try restricting the amount of fluids consumed in the hours before bedtime.

- Think About White Noise: Some people feel that relaxing sounds, such as white noise, can help to create a calming atmosphere for sleeping. This can be particularly helpful if there are outside sounds that might keep you from falling asleep.

Remember that every person has different requirements and preferences, so figuring out which mix of tactics works best for you may require some trial and error. If you are still having trouble falling asleep, speaking with a healthcare provider or a sleep specialist is recommended for additional advice and assessment.

What kind of setting is ideal for restful sleep?

Establishing a sleep-friendly atmosphere is pivotal for encouraging deep, peaceful slumber. Several things Influence an ideal sleeping environment. Here are some pointers for setting up the perfect space for restful sleep:

- Pleasant Pillows and Mattress: Invest in pillows and a comfy mattress that suit your preferences and offer the proper support. Too soft or too hard of a mattress can cause discomfort and interfere with sleep.

- Darkness: Try to keep the bedroom as dark as possible. Consider installing blackout curtains or blinds to prevent external light from interfering with your body's sleep-wake cycle.

- Quietness: Reduce the amount of noise in your bedroom. If necessary, block out distracting noises with white noise generators or earplugs. Establish a calm environment that encourages relaxation.

- Cool Temperature: Keep the room temperature cool. Temperatures between 60 and 67 degrees Fahrenheit (15 and 20 degrees Celsius) are generally considered suitable for sleeping. Generally speaking, cooler temperatures are better for sleeping.

- Ensuring adequate ventilation in the bedroom is crucial. Fresh air helps create a cozy sleeping environment. To increase air circulation, consider opening a window or utilizing a fan.

- Comfy Bedding: Use breathable and cozy bedding materials. Select bedding, blankets, and pajamas made of organic, breathable materials such as cotton. Appropriate bedding can help control body temperature.

- Keep Clocks Out of Sight: If you habitually check the time at night, consider hiding it from view. Checking the time constantly can be stressful and make it difficult to unwind.

- Limit Heavy Meals and Caffeine Before Bed: Avoid coffee and large foods right before bed. Large meals may cause pain, and caffeine is a stimulant that can also interfere with sleep.

- Regular Sleep Schedule: Even on weekends, maintain a regular sleep schedule by going to bed and waking up at the same time each day. The body's internal clock is regulated by consistency.

- Methods of Relaxation: Before bed, engage in relaxation exercises such as deep breathing, meditation, or light stretching. These activities can help with mental relaxation and physiological preparation for sleep.

By incorporating these aspects, you may develop a sleep environment and bedtime routine conducive to sound and peaceful sleep. Try out various tactics to see which one suits you the most, and if your sleep problems don't go away, consider speaking with medical professionals or sleep specialists.

Things to do first when we wake up from sleep.

Your actions can determine your day as soon as you wake up. Consider adopting any of the following wholesome morning routines:

- Exercise Gratitude: Ponder what you must be thankful for a moment. This optimistic outlook can establish the tone for the day.

- Hydrate: After a night of sleep, sip a glass of water to replenish your bodily fluids. This increases your energy and helps your metabolism get going.

- Allow Natural Light to Enter Your Body: Expose yourself to natural light, especially sunlight, as this helps your body know when to get up and regulates your circadian cycle.

- Stretching or Exercise: Do gentle stretching or exercise as part of your morning ritual. This can make you feel more energized and flexible, and have increased blood flow.

- Practice Mindfulness or Meditation: To help you center yourself and develop a peaceful, concentrated mentality, take a few minutes to practice mindfulness, meditation, or deep breathing exercises.

- Eat a Nutritious Breakfast: Fuel your body with a nutritious breakfast. Incorporate a harmonious proportion of fiber, healthy fats and protein in your morning meal.

- Create a Morning Routine: Make sure your morning routine consists of things you enjoy doing every day. This may include spending some time alone before the rigors of the day begin, reading, or keeping a notebook.

- Establish ambitions or goals. Make sure your aspirations for the day are constructive. This might help give your actions emphasis and a sense of direction.

- Avoid Checking Devices Right Away: If you wake up early, consider postponing checking your emails, social media, or news. Give yourself enough time to establish healthy morning routines before stepping into the digital realm.

- Make Your Bed: Although it might not seem like much, making your bed can give you a sense of order and accomplishment and establish a good tone for the rest of the day.

- Individual cleanliness: To feel rejuvenated and ready for the day, practice good hygiene, including cleaning your face and brushing your teeth.

- Organize Your Day: Spend a few minutes organizing your day and reviewing your schedule. Knowing what to expect lets you prioritize your tasks and feel less stressed.

Remember that the activities you select may change depending on your schedule and personal preferences. The aim is to establish a morning routine that supports your well-being and creates a constructive, upbeat atmosphere for the day.

Chapter 8

Navigating Risks: Do's and Don'ts of Risky Substances

Let's see what an alcoholic beverage is.

Technically, the term "alcohol" can apply to various substances; it is most frequently used to identify a family of organic molecules that include a carbon atom bonded to a hydroxyl (-OH) functional group. Ethyl alcohol, or ethanol, is the most widely consumed kind of alcohol by humans and is the primary component of alcoholic beverages.

Yeast ferments sugars, turning them into carbon dioxide and alcohol. This process produces ethanol. Throughout history, people from diverse cultures have drunk alcoholic beverages, including wine, beer, and spirits, which have different ethanol concentrations. They have done this for social, cultural, and recreational purposes.

It's imperative to remember that while some people believe that moderate alcohol use may have health benefits, excessive or careless drinking can hurt one's health and increase the risk of addiction and other social problems. It's important to stress that moderate alcohol consumption is generally understood to mean no more than one drink for women and 2 for men per day. A "drink" is defined as a standard-sized alcoholic beverage with around 14 grams of pure alcohol.

There are various other types of alcohol and some of its advantages. These advantages are not the provoking factors to commence the drink. The purpose of writing this section is that for everything in this universe, there are good and bad associated with it. Now, it's up to the individual how he investigates or looks into it. Some people cannot live without alcohol. We call them "Alcoholic or Bevada," and there are some people who have the facility for drinking but refuse it; such people have solid inner strength, same as "saints or sadhu." Now, it's up to us; we select which feature of our inner self is an "alcoholic or follow like a saints."

Let's get back to the good side of alcohol.

A variety of alcoholic beverages, including wine, spirits, and beer, have differing alcohol contents and possible health advantages. It is noteworthy that moderate alcohol consumption may yield advantages, while excessive alcohol consumption may pose serious health hazards. When used in moderation, the following standard forms of alcoholic beverages may have certain advantages:

Red Wine Advantage: Because it contains antioxidants like resveratrol, red wine is frequently linked to possible cardiovascular benefits. Moderate consumption has been associated with elevated levels of high-density lipoprotein (HDL) cholesterol and may help avoid blood clots.

Beer Benefits: When drunk in moderation, beer may offer cardiovascular advantages comparable to red wine. It may help to increase insulin sensitivity and include certain antioxidants.

White Wine Advantage: White wine, like red wine, has antioxidants and, when drunk in moderation, may benefit the cardiovascular system.

Whiskey: Pertinent research indicates that a moderate intake of alcohol, which includes whiskey, could be linked to a decreased likelihood of specific cardiovascular problems. However, there is more to this topic than just these possible advantages, and there are health dangers to consider.

Benefits of Gin: Moderate gin use has been linked to possible cardiovascular benefits, just like other alcoholic beverages. Juniper berries, one of the botanicals used to make gin, have antioxidant properties.

But it's crucial to consider the possible hazards of alcohol intake, which include a higher chance of addiction, accidents, liver illness, and some types of cancer. For example, because of the hazards involved, the American Heart Association does not advise beginning alcohol consumption purely for cardiovascular advantages.

Before consuming alcohol, people with certain medical illnesses, those with a history of alcohol-related issues, and those using drugs that have harmful interactions with alcohol, should speak with healthcare providers.

Ultimately, each person should decide whether to drink, considering lifestyle, health, and possible hazards.

Consult a healthcare provider if you have any questions or concerns regarding alcohol consumption and its effects on your health.

When alcohol is consumed in excess or for an extended period, it can have a variety of detrimental consequences on the body. The following are some damaging effects of alcohol on the body:

✔ Nervous System in the Center (CNS). Alcohol is a central nervous system depressant that causes depression. It can cause trouble concentrating, slower reaction times, and poor coordination, even in mild doses. When taken in excess, it may cause lethargy, loss of consciousness, or confusion.

✔ The liver metabolizes alcohol; however, excessive alcohol intake can cause fatty liver disease, alcoholic hepatitis, inflammation of the liver, and, ultimately, cirrhosis. One of the leading causes of liver-related health problems is long-term alcohol misuse.

✔ Effects on the Heart: Moderate alcohol use may be beneficial to the heart in some instances, but excessive drinking raises the risk of high blood pressure, arrhythmias, cardiomyopathy (disease of the heart muscle), and heart attacks and strokes.

✔ Immune System Weakness: Extended alcohol consumption can impair immunity, leaving the body more vulnerable to diseases and infections. Long-term alcohol users may be more vulnerable to illnesses, such as respiratory infections.

✔ Problems with the Digestive System: Drinking alcohol can irritate the digestive system, which can result in ulcers, gastritis, and an elevated risk of gastrointestinal bleeding. It may also obstruct the body's ability to absorb nutrients.

✔ Pancreatitis: Excessive alcohol intake may aggravate pancreatic inflammation, a painful illness that can impair digestion and result in life-threatening complications.

✔ Poor Sleep: Although alcohol may work as a sedative at first, it can interfere with the sleep cycle and cause restless nights. It disrupts REM sleep, or rapid eye movement sleep, essential for mental and emotional health.

✔ Increased Cancer Risk: Long-term alcohol consumption has been linked to a higher risk of developing malignancies in several organs, including the mouth, esophagus, liver, and breast.

✔ Mental Health Problems: Depression and anxiety are 2 conditions that alcohol use can intensify. Overindulgence in alcohol consumption can worsen pre-existing mental health issues or promote the emergence of new ones.

✔ Addiction Risk: Alcohol has addictive qualities, and long-term alcohol misuse can result in alcoholism or alcohol use disorders. Addiction can have highly detrimental repercussions on one's social, professional, and personal facets of life.

✔ Social and Professional Consequences: Drinking too much alcohol can have adverse effects on relationships, performance at work, and legal problems, including DUIs (driving while intoxicated).

✔ Alcohol weakens judgment and coordination, which raises the possibility of mishaps and injury. When alcohol is consumed along with tasks like operating machinery or driving, the danger is increased.

It's crucial to remember that everyone reacts differently to alcohol and that the effects of alcohol on the body might vary depending on some variables, including heredity, frequency of usage, overall health, and amount of alcohol consumed. It's best to consult with medical doctors or addiction specialists if you have questions about your alcohol use or how it may be affecting your health.

Herbs (Sheesha), cigarettes, alcohol or electronic cigarettes, all of which pose more significant risks.

When comparing the health hazards of different substances, it is essential to consider several aspects, such as the mode of consumption, frequency of use, and the individual health impacts linked to each substance. The following is a quick summary of the health concerns connected to drinking, e-cigarettes, smoking, and shisha (hookah):

- ✔ The Health Risks of Smoking: Lung cancer, heart disease, other malignancies, respiratory conditions (including emphysema and chronic bronchitis), and other health problems are all significantly influenced by tobacco use. Because of the nicotine content, it is highly addictive.

- ✔ Additional Concerns: Exposure to secondhand smoke might be harmful to non-smokers' health as well.

- ✔ Hookah (shisha): Shisha smokers inhale tobacco smoke through water pipes. Shisha smoking still carries serious health hazards despite the belief held by some that it is less dangerous than smoking cigarettes. It has been linked to heart issues, lung conditions, and a higher chance of developing several types of cancer. The social aspect of hookah use may also facilitate infectious disease transmission.

- ✔ Myth: Shisha smoking may be just as hazardous, if not more so, than cigarette smoking, due to the incomplete filtration of dangerous components in the vapor by the water in the hookah.

- ✔ Alcohol: Dangers to Health: Several health hazards, including liver disease, cardiovascular problems, an increased risk of accidents and injuries, addiction (alcohol use disorder), and an increased risk of some malignancies, are linked to excessive alcohol intake. While there may be cardiovascular benefits to moderate alcohol use, excessive drinking has significant health hazards.

✔ Alcohol can also have an impact on judgment and behavior, which can lead to risky behavior and social problems.

✔ Health Concerns with E-Cigarettes: Instead of using traditional smoke to deliver nicotine, e-cigarettes, also known as vaping devices, use an aerosol. Although vaping is frequently promoted as a less hazardous option to smoking, its long-term health effects are yet unclear. Even with their potential for dangerous drug content, e-cigarettes can cause lung damage (such as vaping-associated lung injury or EVALI) and other health risks.

✔ Concerns Regarding Youth Use: Youth e-cigarette use has increased, which has sparked worries about nicotine addiction and possible long-term health consequences.

It's crucial to remember that all of these substances have health dangers, and the best way to safeguard your health is through complete abstinence. Furthermore, different people may react differently to various medications, and some may be more vulnerable to health problems than others.

How can we give up smoking and alcohol?

Now, when people already have a habit of drinking or smoking, it seems complicated to advise people to quit. People think as if someone is lecturing, and why he is bothering. "I am drinking/smoking from my own earned money. I am not borrowing from you, so why are you having pain?" This is the statement I have heard from my best friend. I assume the same may happen with everyone who wants their friends/spouse to quit this bad habit.

Although giving up alcohol and tobacco can be difficult, doing so is a healthy and constructive move for your well-being. The following general advice could be helpful to you during the process:

- ✔ Giving Up Alcohol:,

  - ○ Establish Specific Objectives:

  - ○ Clarify your motivation for quitting and make quantifiable, precise goals.

  - ○ Seek Support: Talk to your loved ones about your decision so they can offer you support and understanding.

  - ○ Expert Assistance: Consider obtaining assistance from a medical practitioner or a therapist with expertise in addiction treatment.,

  - ○ Avoid Triggers: Recognize and stay away from people or situations that make you want to drink.

  - ○ Create a Support System: Connect with people in comparable situations by joining support groups or locating a sober community.

  - ○ Create Healthy Habits: Instead of drinking, engage in hobbies, physical activity, or socializing in non-alcoholic environments.

  - ○ Stress management and mindfulness: To deal with stress without drinking, use stress management and mindfulness practices.

  - ○ Celebrate Milestones: To reaffirm your dedication, commemorate your victories along the route.

- ✔ Giving Up Smoking:

  - ○ Setting a Quit Date for Smoking: Decide on a specific date to stop smoking and psychologically prepare for it.

  - ○ Nicotine Replacement Therapy (NRT): To help control withdrawal symptoms, consider using nicotine replacement products, such as gum, patches, or lozenges.

  - ○ Prescription Drugs: Speak with a medical expert about prescription drugs that could aid in quitting smoking.

  - ○ Behavioral Therapy: To address the psychological aspects of smoking addiction, seek out behavioral therapy or counseling.

  - ○ Steer clear of triggers:

  - ○ Recognize and stay away from situations that make you want to smoke.

  - ○ Stay Active: To assist in managing stress and enhance your general well-being, get frequent exercise.

  - ○ Healthy Diet: Keep a healthy diet to promote general health and reduce weight gain from quitting smoking.

  - ○ Establish a Support Network:

Talk to your loved ones about your objective, and enlist the help of individuals who have successfully given up smoking.

Recall that each person's path is distinct, and asking for expert assistance when necessary is acceptable. Seek individualized aid and help from healthcare practitioners or addiction specialists if you are struggling to quit on your own.

Chapter 9

Financial Wellness: Managing Money for a Secure Future

Various factors, including individual health issues, lifestyle choices, access to healthcare, and geographic location, can significantly affect the expense of maintaining good health. Determining a precise "bare minimum" cost for optimal health is challenging because health-related costs can encompass medical treatments, preventive care, prescription drugs, food, exercise, and mental wellness etc.

But, let's talk about some broad health-related cost considerations:

- ✔ Prevention of Care: Preventive screenings and routine examinations are crucial for preserving excellent health. Although preventive care can be expensive, it includes regular checkups, immunizations, and testing for diabetes, heart disease, and cancer.

- ✔ Health Insurance: Health insurance is essential for controlling medical expenses. The price of health insurance can vary dramatically depending on several variables, including coverage, deductibles, copayments, and plan type. The total cost may also vary depending on your access to government programs, individual plans, or employer-sponsored insurance. Your insurance premium will be more if you are not fit and healthy.

- ✔ Nutrition: A healthy, well-balanced diet and nutrient-rich diet is essential. The price of food can change depending on a person's diet, the cost of goods in their area economy inflation, and whether they select processed, fresh or organic. items.

✔ Physical Activity: Regular physical activity enhances well-being in general. Exercise classes, gym memberships, and outdoor activities are some expenses linked to physical activity.

✔ Mental Health: Mental health is an essential element of total well-being. Treatment for mental health issues may involve psychiatric services, therapy, or counseling. Furthermore, practicing mindfulness or other mental health-promoting activities can be expensive.

✔ Prescription drug costs can account for a sizable portion of overall healthcare costs. The type of medication, insurance coverage, and the availability of generic alternatives are some of the factors that affect prescription expenses.

✔ Unplanned and Emergency Medical Costs: Unexpected medical problems or crises can occur, resulting in unanticipated healthcare expenses. A financial resource or emergency reserve can manage unexpected costs.

✔ Dental and Ocular Health: Taking care of your teeth and eyesight is crucial to your general health. Consider the costs of dental exams, cleanings, eyeglasses and contact lenses.

It is noteworthy that long-term cost reductions in healthcare can be achieved through investing in healthy lifestyle practices, early intervention, and preventive interventions. Making lifestyle choices that prioritize health can positively impact overall well-being, while some costs cannot be avoided.

Ultimately, people should consider their health needs, speak with medical professionals, and make well-informed decisions tailored to their interests and circumstances. There may be differences in the availability of inexpensive healthcare and services, so it can be helpful to ask for financial guidance or help when necessary.

With this perspective, you can follow the steps outlined in chapters 1 through 8 to achieve holistic wellness or to secure financial resources for future health needs

Chapter 10

Beyond the Scale: Sustaining Weight Loss and Embracing Mindfulness

Here are mindfulness techniques to sustain weight loss and essential beliefs to keep and preserve excellent health:

- Eating a diet rich in whole grains, lean meats, fruits, veggies, and healthy fats will give you a good balance of nutrients. Reduce your consumption of processed foods, added sugars and salt.

- Frequent Exercise: Exercise regularly to improve your flexibility, strength, and cardiovascular health. In addition to muscle-strengthening activities, try to get in at least 180 minutes of moderate-intensity, or 90 minutes of vigorous-intensity exercise per week.

- Sufficient Hydration: Consume enough water throughout the day to stay hydrated. Water is necessary for several body processes, such as nutrition transfer, temperature regulation, and digestion.

- Adequate Sleep: Prioritize adequate and high-quality sleep. Try to get between 7 to 9 hours each night for your general health, mental clarity, and emotional stability.

- Stress Management: Use stress-reduction methods, including yoga, mindfulness, meditation, and deep breathing. Long-term stress can be detrimental to one's physical and emotional well-being.

- Frequent Medical Examinations: Make time for routine checkups with medical professionals so that you can receive immunizations and preventive screenings. Early recognition of health problems can result in more successful interventions.

- Health Monitoring: Pay attention to any changes in your body's condition. Follow your doctor's advice and monitor blood pressure, cholesterol, and blood sugar levels.

- Moderate Alcohol Consumption: If you decide to drink, do it cautiously.

- Refrain from Smoking and Reduce Tobacco Exposure: Refrain from smoking and reduce your exposure to secondhand smoke. One of the most significant risk factors for several illnesses, such as cardiovascular and respiratory disorders, is smoking.

- Social Networks: Establish and preserve social networks. A robust social support system and wholesome relationships are essential for mental and emotional health.

- Mental Health Care: Make mental health a priority by practicing self-care, getting professional assistance when necessary, and striking a healthy work-life balance.

- Preventive actions: Use sunscreen, maintain proper hygiene, and adhere to safety precautions to reduce the likelihood of illnesses and accidents.

- Ongoing Education: Make informed decisions and keep up with health-related subjects. Continue your education regarding fitness, diet, and other facets of health.

- Maintain a Healthy Weight: A balanced diet and frequent exercise will help you reach and stay healthy. Seek advice from medical professionals for specific recommendations.

- Cut Down on Screen Time: Cut back on too much screen time, especially right before bed. This includes gadgets such as laptops, tablets, and smartphones. Better sleep quality is supported by getting enough screen time.

Recall that maintaining good health is a lifetime process, and everyone has different needs. Adjust these guidelines to your situation and get individual advice from medical professionals. Gradual, sustainable adjustments can enhance long-term health and well-being.

About The Book

In *10 Paths to Uncover Wellness,* readers embark on a journey toward a healthier and more fulfilling life. The introduction chapter, "Finding Purpose" establishes the tone by urging people to identify their deep purpose, which fosters the drive required for meaningful and lasting change.

The following chapters act as secrets that dig into many aspects of well-being. Beginning with "Importance of Social Relationships," it addresses the profound impact of human relationships on mental and emotional health. The book then switches its focus to practical issues, with chapters on "Time Management," "Diet Management," and "Workout chapters giving readers the tools they need to manage their daily routines for better physical and mental health.

Recognizing the widespread nature of stress in modern life, "Stress Management" provides ways for dealing with and reducing stressors. "Sleep Management" emphasizes the need for enough Sleep and general well-being.

Addressing critical lifestyle choices, "Do's and Don'ts of Risky Substances" offers guidance on making informed decisions regarding substances that can affect health. "Financial Management" explores the connection between financial well-being and overall wellness, emphasizing that the cost of maintaining a healthy lifestyle is ultimately lower than the cumulative expenses of an unhealthy one.

The book finishes with "Sustaining Weight Loss and Mindful Techniques," which provides practical advice for sustaining progress and applying mindfulness to daily life.

"10 Paths to Uncover Wellness" is a comprehensive guide to personal development, designed to help readers achieve a balanced work-life dynamic and lead more fulfilling lives.

About The Author

JS Kumar is a Project Management Consultant with nearly two decades of experience in the Oil & Gas industry and holds a degree in Engineering and Master's in Business Administration. He specializes in Project Management Techniques, including Planning, Cost Control, Risk Management, Contract Administration, Procurement Management, Monitoring, Reporting, etc. As an entrepreneur, he has started several start-ups and is a people health expert with learning from Harvard Medical School and Robert Simic Coaching Institute about NLP, Life Coach & Hypnotism. Living overseas with his family, he loves communicating with people from different cultures.

Kumar is passionate about lifelong learning, especially in technology and psychology, and is known for supporting individuals and organizations with Stress Management, Project Management, Lifestyle Consultancy, and Work-life balance.

He is pursuing a career in psychology and the Unconventional Oil & Gas business to enhance his personal and professional well-being.

Let's connect to build a balanced life together.

Email: info@centricenergy.llc

Before

After